home to HOLLYWOOD

A Practical Guide to Establishing Yourself in Los Angeles

CELINE WALLACE

ILLUSTRATIONS BY MELISSA MOLINA

AuthorHouse™
1663 Liberty Drive
Bloomington, IN 47403
www.authorhouse.com
Phone: 1-800-839-8640

Published by AuthorHouse 02/27/14

ISBN: 978-1-4918-6611-5 (sc)
ISBN: 978-1-4918-6612-2 (e)

Any people depicted in stock imagery provided by Thinkstock are models,
and such images are being used for illustrative purposes only.
Certain stock imagery © Thinkstock.

This book is printed on acid-free paper.

Because of the dynamic nature of the Internet, any web addresses or links contained in
this book may have changed since publication and may no longer be valid. The views
expressed in this work are solely those of the author and do not necessarily reflect the
views of the publisher, and the publisher hereby disclaims any responsibility for them.

authorHOUSE®

★ ★

ABOUT

Celine Wallace is a Los Angeles based, New Zealand born actress. She has been performing since the age of 7 and has developed a successful career in entertainment that led her to America. Celine is currently a working SAG-AFTRA actress, as well as a writer and voice-over artist with a Bachelor's degree in Performing and Screen Arts. Celine has experience as a casting associate for Hollywood casting director Julie Ashton of Warner Bros. She is about to start shooting her next feature film in Detroit as this book enters publication.

★ ★

CONTENTS

Whether you are already established or just starting out, congratulations—you are making the move to Los Angeles to pursue a professional career in acting. I applaud you. It's a wonderful thing to have a dream, and setting out to fulfill it requires courage.

In saying this, becoming an actor in Hollywood isn't easy. A lot of young, hopeful actors think that it's effortless and that becoming famous is simple. That's probably because we live in a society where people can become famous for doing absolutely nothing. But one thing you have to take seriously—something that most people won't tell you but all people in the business know—is that acting is a skill that requires a lot of work. It's something that people take very seriously, especially all the people you're working with or trying to get to hire you. Each year, thousands of actors move to California with hopes of making it big. Some don't succeed, but while the odds of becoming a big film or television star are low, it is still possible, so we want to improve your chances. To do that, before you move, you need to have all that you can set up. This way, you can settle in quicker, focus on your career, and focus on establishing yourself.

The world of Hollywood is a mysterious one, and you hear stories of "lucky" girls being discovered on the street. Please don't move yourself across the country or across the world with the hope that you may be one of these "lucky" ones. Most of the time, luck exists in the form of being in the right place and equally prepared. Perhaps you're preparing to head to LA and need to be prepared, or maybe you've already made the leap of faith. Whatever the case, throughout this book we are going to give you a plan and make sure you always think of yourself as the rule and never the exception. By doing this, we already help to protect you from disappointment. The majority of people I have seen fail have lacked preparation, and Hollywood has no pity for the weak of heart or pocket.

When I first moved to Los Angeles, I looked for such a book as I have written here to help guide me on my path, but I wasn't able to find one. After many trials and errors, I decided to write one myself. I want to give you a shortcut, and I don't want you to make the same, often-expensive and/or time-consuming mistakes.

In the following chapters of this book, we will cover all the essential tools you will need to get started, from housing to headshots and everything in between. If you feel some of the information covered in a specific section doesn't serve you then feel free to move onto the content that applies to you. The goal of this book is to help you be successful, both as a person and as an actor, so actively use it and carry it in your bag as your practical go-to guide to establishing yourself in the entertainment industry in Los Angeles. Though before we get started, please do me a favor: don't have false expectations for this book—there is no model for Tinseltown.

The industry is forever changing, the talent pool is constantly growing older, and new, fresh actors are constantly joining the market. Therefore, this book is in a constant state of revision. This is an extremely competitive business, but with the right guidance, it is a fun journey—a journey in which I believe if you can dream it, you can achieve it. I hope some of the information in the following pages can help you facilitate achieving your dreams.

> *Someone might have a germ of talent, but 90 per cent of it is discipline and how you practice it, what you do with it. Instinct won't carry you through the entire journey. It's what you do in the moments between inspiration. The film industry is so noisy … but the noise doesn't interest me—the work does.*
>
> —Cate Blanchett, Golden Globe and Academy Award Winning Actress

The very basic survival tools you will need to get started include an apartment, a car, a state driver's license, a day job, some savings, and a bank account (if you are foreign). These are the bare minimum survival tools. Almost every industry professional I have come into contact with has recommended that you have enough savings to live for two years without any income if you are trying to break into the acting business.

A DAY JOB

Because it can be difficult until you are established, it's important to have what is often called a day job, which is something you do to keep your bills paid while you audition for acting jobs. There are a number of types of day jobs, from telemarketing and food service to the more career-oriented ones like teaching and production services. Most popular day jobs and/or careers tend to be self-employed positions, because this allows you to have flexibility around your auditions and create your own schedule. Popular jobs in this vein are personal trainers or positions in hospitality (such as a waiter, hostess, or bartender). Hospitality positions in particular are good because you usually work nights, which leaves days free to audition.

There is no right or wrong day job; this job is fundamentally there to help you pay your bills so you can still audition and not end up on the streets. For example, I found my day job because I love fitness. Ever since I was a kid, I would play every sport I could think of. I started trying all these different types of exercise and found I had a passion for Pilates. I saved up and participated in a workshop to become certified, started approaching studios, and within a few months began teaching.

I do this on the side of my acting when I'm not working on a full-time project, and it's almost a treat because I get to share something else I'm passionate about. The fact that I am doing something I enjoy and am passionate about feeds back into my art, and as an added bonus, I don't resent going to work. Living in LA, I've especially noticed that it's important to have a day job you enjoy, because so many actors get burnt out working horrible jobs and then auditioning all day.

Nothing is work unless you'd rather be doing something else.

—George Halas, nicknamed "Mr. Everything" was a player, coach, owner, and pioneer in professional American football

During my research, I interviewed Warner Bros. writer and television show creator Zak Shaikh and asked him what he considered important investments when he first moved to Los Angeles. His response was as follows:

It's essential to invest in finding a source of income that is not based on entertainment or artistic ventures. Whether that's getting a real estate license or teaching Pilates or becoming a plumber. Make sure that other work has some flexibility to it so it doesn't take you entirely away from your main artistic goals. I also think investing in a nice place to live can make a difference. A lot of people think that doesn't matter, but waking up in a place where you feel happy, rather than on someone's sofa in West Hollywood can help. That said, there are plenty of stories of artists who live completely bohemian, temporary, and unstable lives who go on to succeed. So don't listen to me. - Zak Shaikh (Writer, Warner Bros) in discussion, 2013.

This leads me to my next point.

HOUSING

Housing is something you should try to set up before you arrive so you have somewhere to settle in. There are tons of websites that offer listings in California; Craigslist and Westside Rentals are the main two. Craigslist is free, while Westside Rentals is membership based. It is a good idea to arrange a temporary place to stay in the first week while you set up viewings of all the apartments in the areas within your budget. Most apartments require a one-year lease, so be prepared to find an apartment you can afford for that year or two.

You want to spend the first one to two years establishing yourself rather than relocating repeatedly. When you first move in, you will be required to undergo a credit check, where the landlord will check your credit history. If you don't own a credit card or are new to the United States, this might be an issue, because you won't have a credit history. You may be able to get around this by providing your landlord security in other ways by showing evidence of bank statements, giving extra rent up front, or paying a double security deposit until you establish your credit history.

For example, in my case, I was lucky in that my landlord said I could pay the first and last months' rent as security in addition to the standard security deposit for damages. I encourage you to ask your landlord to see if he would be willing to do something similar—it never hurts to ask. If you don't want to sign a lease and have no credit history, the best thing to do would be to sublet a room, apartment, or shared flat with someone who is going away. The best place to find sublets is on Craigslist, and most subleased apartments come furnished as well.

If you are signing a lease and need furniture, there are several good resources. IKEA has a great selection of new, cheap, and contemporary furniture. On Craigslist, you can find new and re-used furniture (often being resold by people who are relocating). If you are after more vintage furniture, antiques, or consignment items, try out some of California's great flea markets. Two of the best are Melrose Trading Post, which is every Sunday at Fairfax High School on Melrose and Fairfax; or The Rose Bowl Flea Market, which is on the second Sunday of every month in Pasadena, California.

When selecting a place to live, pick somewhere you can be relaxed, because, trust me, you will value a relaxing and comfortable environment. LA is nicknamed "the melting pot," which means it is known for experiencing every type of person from every walk of life. It is inevitable that some days will be manic. I especially value my peace and quiet at home if I have a casting the next day and want to prepare my lines. Some actors I've known have moved to California, slept on a couch or in a house with crazy parties every night, and were never able to learn their lines. I'm sad to say that they haven't lasted very long. For this reason, it's important to consider the bigger picture when searching for housing.

In terms of exactly where to move when first coming to LA, Hollywood is where you will find most of the casting studios and agencies. For this reason, a lot of actors move to Hollywood or West Hollywood for the first year to become familiar with the city. Then, when they are more established and have a manager or agent, they will consider moving farther out, often to the beach cities like Santa Monica or Malibu. There are also good neighborhood pockets around Hollywood; Los Feliz, Studio City, Burbank, and Mid-Wilshire are all centrally located around Hollywood but more residential.

CARS

Once you are here for good, you will need to buy a car—something that can get you from point A to point B. Transportation in LA is a topic of debate for many people, and a lot of actors come to LA and bus or train their way to auditions. You can get around LA without a car; you can also eat cereal without a spoon, but it's not a pleasant experience and is time consuming and messy. It's a well-known fact that the public transportation system in Los Angeles is less than adequate and not always reliable; add in the component of traffic, and it is generally a nightmare.

If you are planning on going to one audition a week and allowing two hours of traveling time either side of your audition call time, which is not including traffic, then by all means, consider using the bus system an option. If you are expecting to be a professional actor who will sometimes be attending as many as four or six castings a day, you will need a car. You don't need a flashy or expensive car, just a basic car to get you from point A to point B. If your credit history is an issue, you should consider buying a car using financing, which is a great way to slowly build up your credit history. It's a win-win situation.

BUYING A CAR

Three of the most commonly used resources for buying cars are Craigslist (which usually has private sales, so it can be cheaper), CarMax (a trusted car dealership with prices that aren't too expensive and a range of different vehicles with car service and history reports), or Nick Alexander Imports (a private dealership that deals in brand-new cars). Keep in mind that when moving to LA, you will spend more time in your car than anywhere else. It's almost more important than were you live - you don't want it breaking down on your way to an audition.

RENTING VERSUS LEASING A CAR

If you aren't ready to invest in a car, another great alternative is renting a car, which you can organize online before you arrive. Avis, Budget, Enterprise, and Hertz are four of the biggest providers, and they also have stations at the airport so you can pick up your rental car and drive straight to your destination once you touch down. Just keep in mind that if you plan to remain in LA permanently, you will eventually need to invest in a vehicle.

Leasing a car is also an option and very reliable because all of the maintenance is free, and the car can be completely taken care of. The only negative with leasing a car is that at the end of that lease, you have no car and have spent all that money when you could have invested in something long-term. Everyone's opinion is different, but in my opinion, if you buy a car, then you have something you can sell in the end and possibly try to get a percentage of your initial money invested back.

If none of the above options are open to you because you are really on a budget and need a car, there is a used-car rental company called Rent-A-Wreck that has a range of different cars, some wrecks, some not. However, all of the fleet is clean and inspected to make sure your safety isn't compromised.

When I moved to Los Angeles, I wasn't ready to invest much in a vehicle, so rented for a week, went through Craigslist postings, and drove around looking at all the potential private-sale cars. I ended up buying a 2000 Volkswagen Beetle for three thousand dollars, which was a bargain. Of course, the downside was that I had to stand in line at the DMV for four hours to change over all the paperwork.

Unfortunately, my cute little bug had a lot of mechanical problems, and after a year, it broke down beyond repair. Then it was time to make a decision. I was sick of having my car at the mechanic all the time and decided to invest in a car. I wanted one that wouldn't give me problems, and so I spent a considerable amount more. I love my car and now have the security of having it under a warranty. If anything goes wrong, I have people to help me 24/7.

Please don't read this and think I'm suggesting you buy a brand-new, fancy car that stretches you beyond your means or for you to run out and apply for a loan. You will need as much money as possible to help you maintain living expenses while pursing your acting dream. Just take in all this information and assess which category works best for you. Who knows, maybe you do what I did—a private-sale car first and then upgrade later on. Either way you'll make the right decision for you.

DRIVER'S LICENSE

Once you have gotten a car, getting your license is the next step. You need your license, because in addition to making it legal to be on the road, it provides you with a California State ID. To get this you must take a two-part test at the DMV (Department of Motor Vehicles), consisting of both a written and practical exam. You can then use your driver's license as a form of ID everywhere in California, so it eliminates the need to carry around your normal state ID or passport.

You should do this as soon as possible, because you will likely be able to purchase cheaper car insurance, as you will be considered less of a risk to the insurance company. Keep in mind that to get a Californian license you need a Social Security number. If you're foreign and have come here on a visitor's visa to try your luck in Hollywood, you won't be eligible to apply for a license. However, you will be able to obtain a general Californian State ID, which you also apply for at the DMV. For this application, you will need two forms of identification, usually your passport, working visa, or birth certificate.

You can find out more information about obtaining either a California driver's license or state ID online at the DMV website: http://www.dmv.ca.gov/portal/home/dmv.htm.

PARKING TICKETS

LA is known for its notorious parking tickets from the relentless parking wardens. In this city, if you leave your car meter expired by literally *one* minute, you are pretty much guaranteed to come back to your car with the disgusting sight of a rectangular slip of paper tucked under your wiper. There's also the weekly street sweeping schedule, so be mindful of the signs when you park on the street. Tickets costs can cost $63, $68, $93, or more—and double that if you pay late, so it's not a mistake you want (or can afford) to make.

Most meters accept credit cards or quarters, and meter parking generally costs between one and three dollars, depending on the time and area. (For example, Beverly Hills will probably charge you more, because, after all, it's Beverly Hills.) But seriously, three dollars is better than sixty-eight dollars, so don't skimp on the meters—you will regret it.

SAVINGS AND BANK ACCOUNTS

If you grew up in America, it's likely you already have a bank account, so that's one less thing you need to organize. However, it's important to ensure you're prepared with enough savings for your move and initial setup. As I mentioned previously, most industry professionals recommended you have at least two years' worth of savings that you can budget to live off of.

It's possible, but unlikely, that you will book professional work upon landing, and finding the right day job may take awhile. If you want to be selective about what work you get into, it's essential to have some financial backing. Make sure you're coming out to Los Angeles with enough to cover your rent, food, utilities, and transportation expenses. In the event you do find work quickly, it will be an added bonus to have your savings. Who knows, maybe you could treat yourself to a vacation.

If you don't already have an American bank account, it will be important to do so. To open an account, you need to have a Social Security number, proof of address (bills, a lease, or other document with your address and name on it), and a photo ID (driver's license and/or passport). If you don't have one of these items, most importantly a Social Security number, you will not be able to open an account.

Your Social Security number (often referred to as simply your Social) is your government identification number that says you're legally allowed to work in the United States. Without this, the bank often assumes you're unable to legally work, which leads to the question of why you would need a bank account. If you have your documents, work permit, and Social, the process is simply. If you don't have your Social or are waiting for it to come through, you may still be able to open an account through Washington Mutual. This bank works on an individual basis, meaning if you get a friendly clerk who decides they like you, then you're set. If you get a clerk on a bad day, then you're out of luck—welcome to America.

If you are just waiting on your Social Security number to come through (which can take one week or one month, depending on processing), I would recommend waiting to open a bank account. I know it can be frustrating to wait, but it's best to use one of the major banks. They offer better setups and are more easily accessible. Some good corporate banks include Bank of America, Chase Bank, and Wells Fargo.

This chapter has included a lot of information about your initial setup. I hope you're still convinced to head to the City of Angels. Just take everything onboard and position yourself for success with proper planning and the basics covered here.

Now let's get down to the business of acting. Behold five elemental items that belong in your carry-on bag long before you pack your sunscreen—your acting tools. These "tools," as they will be referred to in this chapter, consist of your headshot, résumé, reels, and website.

I would try encouraging anyone wanting to pursue a career in acting in Hollywood to make the move when you have momentum from a few high-profile bookings, film festivals, or hits on a web series. Try to generate some buzz before you come to LA, so when you meet with people in the business, you have experience and a portfolio to show them. Then know your plan when you hit the ground. Don't think you can wing it and be discovered at the local Starbucks.

Don't worry, though, if you don't already have some credits; there are other options. For example, you can try finding some reputable acting schools in Hollywood and get that on your résumé. Go to casting director workshops and get in front of casting directors so they become familiar with you. Ask them questions and start gaining exposure for yourself. Also ask around your connections in your hometown before you leave. Old acting coaches or schools, talent agents, and casting directors often have connections in Hollywood, so they may be able to help you land representation. Or who knows, they might even help you get a foot in the door at the top casting offices.

A friend of mine befriended a director on location years earlier that ended up recommending him to a top manager upon arrival, and then he was set. Just make sure you understand that if you don't have a few solid credits on your résumé, you will have to work even harder than the average Joe.

HEADSHOTS

An actor's headshot is his business card, and a picture is worth a thousand words as the saying goes. First and foremost, your headshot needs to look like you. It should look like you but reflect you in the best possible manner while not being forced or posed.

It needs to be professionally produced, and many actors hire professional makeup artists. However, it's important to keep in mind that you don't want it to be forced or posed, because an overly glamorized look will only inhibit your chances. A professional makeup artist usually understands this concept and will have a fair idea of the look to achieve while minimizing cosmetic imperfections and bringing out your natural appeal. By focusing on your natural appeal, you are being more yourself and more versatile for a wider range of different roles.

During the photo editing process, remember this: you need to look like the person in the head-shot, so do not get your shot so retouched or done with makeup that it's unrealistic. If that happens, even if you do get in the room, you won't look like the person in the photograph. That can be a waste of everyone's time and is also annoying for the casting director.

In regards to logistics, headshots should be a vertical eight-by-ten-inch photo with or without borders and with or without your name on the front. I recommend including a border and print-ing your name on the front of your picture, just underneath the border. This is the most common way to display a headshot.

Most actors have multiple headshots for different categories they are submitting for. If you were submitting for a theatrical project, you would use something more natural and dramatic. A commercial headshot tends to be smiling and playful; these commercial shots can also be used for projects other than commercials, such as a television comedy pilot where the charac-ters are more playful and upbeat. Once you have decided which photographs you are going to use for each category, have them duplicated at a photo lab. LA has many photo labs that cater to actors, and you can easily find options closest to you through the Internet. You'll usually need about one hundred of these photographs, and you can often negotiate a cheaper rate if you get more printed.

Dana Patrick of Dana Patrick Photography is the go-to girl for the top agencies in Hollywood for headshots. She photographs many of the entertainment industry's brightest stars, including actors, musicians, and models. I asked Dana what she would say to an actor coming to Los Angeles prior to getting headshots taken.

The following is her advice:

> I would say prior to getting headshots taken that they should go online and check out actors' headshots. Many of the actors that I have spoken to as to why they chose me said that they did just this, and most of the shots they liked were ours. Also, to know that headshots are very subjective and *everyone* has "their" phi-losophy as to what works. Go with someone that you feel will make you stand out amongst the crowds. This, I feel, is a way to get a potential agent's attention whether they like the shot or not. Vanilla and safe will only make you unmemora-ble—again, just *my* opinion.

The key mistake actors make with headshots—this happens to be a mistake oftentimes made due to an agent's directions—trying to be photographed as every type within your age range. It looks ridiculous and amateur to play characters. I feel an actor looks more polished and like a "real" actor when they allude to their casting and bring a part of themselves to the overall styling so that they own their shot and the characters that they might play, as opposed to looking like everyone else within their category. If everyone is sending in the same exact shot to a casting director for a certain type of character, it only seems like common sense that this is not only mind numbing for casting but that they simply just want to find their "girl next door," and if your shot says "girl next door" but is a little more unique and stands out, I feel that you just made their job easier to find you. – Dana Patrick (Headshot photographer, Dana Patrick Photography) in discussion, 2013.

Here are some of Dana's examples of the "girl next door" look and how it varies for each unique person while still being in the same category.

To find out more about booking with Dana you can check out her website at: http://www.da-napatrick.com.

RÉSUMÉS

Your résumé should highlight your best roles and experiences and should be no longer than one page. Even the best actors in the world narrow their résumés down to one page. If they can do it, you should be able to too. When you flip a headshot over, a résumé should be stapled to the back, and one staple is sufficient (don't go crazy). Another common mistake is printing your résumé on the back of your headshot. Your résumé will need to be updated, and the pictures won't always be valid, so you want to keep things simple.

Printing these résumés and headshots can be expense, but it's worth the investment because this is your calling card. Before you even get in the audition room, this is the first thing that a casting department sees; otherwise, you may not get in the audition room.

At the top of your résumé you will need your full name, and under that, be sure to list if you are a union member—for example, SAG-AFTRA (more on unions later). The next item that may seem obvious but that a lot of people forget is contact information, so, essentially, your representation. If you don't have representation, your contact information would be your e-mail address and best contact phone number. If you do have representation, you don't list you personal contact information, because an employer only needs your personal information once you have booked the job. If you list both your representation's information and your personal information, it can come across as amateur or unprofessional.

Your résumé is then broken into three sections: work, training, and skills. The first subcategory on your résumé for work is experience and should be listed in this order: film, television, and then theatre. What you don't list on your theatrical résumé are commercials, modeling, and print jobs. If you are new and starting out, list whatever you've done, and if you've done nothing in one of those categories, leave the category off and work slowly on building it up. Don't freak out if you don't have something in a category or if it's small. Everyone has to start somewhere; just make sure you don't fabricate your résumé. Be honest and build it up.

The second section should be training. Aim to show a variety of training to establish diversity, such as scene study class, improv, audition techniques, and workshops. You can list it all and then shop around and train with some credible Hollywood acting coaches or acting studios.

You can then list those on your résumé as a starting point if you don't have any significant credits. That way, casting directors can look at names they recognize and gain a level of association of who you've worked with and possibly what your style or skill level is.

The third and final section on your résumé should be skills. You need to list every practical skill that you've mastered that could be used in production. For instance, horse riding, bartending, surfing, swimming, and driving are skills often required in film and television. Make sure any skill you claim you can perform on your résumé you can do to a good standard to convince the audience. Don't say something for the sake of it and get caught, because that would be not only awkward for you but for casting as well.

JOHN DOE
PLACE EMAIL HERE
PLACE PHONE HERE

FILM

Project Title	Role/Position	Company/Director

TELEVISION

Project Title	Role/Position	Company/Director

THEATRE

Project Title	Role/Position	Company/Director

COMMERICAL

(Full list available and conflicts available on request)

TRAINING

Project Title	Role/Position	Company/Director

SPECIAL SKILLS

General:
Dance:
Dialects:
Sports:
Stunts:
Other experience:

REPRESENTATION

LOGO

JOHN DOE
SAG/AFTRA

FILM

Project Title	Role/Position	Company/Director

TELEVISION

Project Title	Role/Position	Company/Director

THEATRE

Project Title	Role/Position	Company/Director

COMMERICAL

(Full list available and conflicts available on request)

TRAINING

Project Title	Role/Position	Company/Director

SPECIAL SKILLS

General:
Dance:
Dialects:
Sports:
Stunts:
Other experience:

REELS

A demo reel is similar to a résumé, except in video form. A reel is a compilation of scenes of professional work you've done that can be used to show a casting director or agent your range and skill set as an actor. This is essential, because the entertainment industry is a visual medium. It shows proof of the work you've done and also confirms your acting ability. One of the common questions people have is regarding how long it should be. You want to keep your reel short, usually two minutes max, and put your most interesting work at the beginning to hook in the viewer. Keep in mind that it takes thirty seconds to make an impression.

There are companies that will help you produce your reel; you take them the raw footage of your scenes, and they cut them together. You can also cut your reel together yourself; just make sure you have a good understanding of what you want to create so it looks as professional as possible. A great, fast and reliable professional demo reel editing company is Planet Video, so I would recommend checking them out if you have raw footage. You might like to make multiple versions of your demo too so you can provide a tape specifically for a certain style of acting or type of position. It's important to match the content to the position you're applying for.

Most people have two reels, one dramatic reel and one comedic reel. Obviously, they are very different styles, so if you're applying for a dramatic role, you wouldn't send in your reel displaying how well you do comedy. If you're just starting out and have a combination of both but nothing long enough for two minutes of each, put together your best footage. In that case, it's okay to put them together.

If you don't have any footage to create a reel, don't stress. You can self-submit for projects online and build up your portfolio with unpaid projects. Student projects are often good to do this with; however, they can go either way in terms of quality. Actors I know have also gotten together with friends or other actors to film scenes, but unless footage is shot professionally, I would recommend waiting to put together your reel until you have some professional footage. You have probably also heard of companies that you can pay to develop and record professional-looking footage for you. In my opinion, this can be a gamble, because they range in quality depending on the company and generally cost a lot of money.

I would then personally wait until you have professional footage to use instead of paying for expensive services. In the meantime, self-submit for student projects to get footage that is free. If you are inclined to use a company to produce scenes for your reel, I recommend Rapid Reelz in Los Angeles. They are on the more expensive side but produce high-quality and professional-looking footage, so you know you are getting what you pay for.

Ultimately, the rule is quality over quantity. You want evidence you have worked, but you don't want it to be poor quality, because it will just make you look unprofessional and inhibit your chances instead of increasing them.

Reels are a great way to showcase your skills, but if you don't have the footage, then you don't have it. That's it. Just work on building your résumé, and your footage will come as a by-product of that.

WEBSITES

Actor websites are another tool to help you market yourself in the industry. In my opinion, they are not essential, but many people in the industry have different views on this. True, they are good to have so you can have a place you can put all of your material and post information that is easily accessible to casting directors and agents. A major casting director or agent has never asked me for a website, and when I was a casting associate for Warner Bros., I don't recall a time I looked at one. The likelihood of casting looking at your website is small, because they are given headshots and résumés and usually only look at reels if they need validation and are unsure. Most casting offices just don't have time.

If you want to create a website, it won't hurt, but I wouldn't pay to have one made. There are lots of website hosting services, such as Squarespace and GoDaddy, so take advantage of these services where you can build your own website and manage it yourself. If you decide to take this route, the content on an actor's website generally consists of photos, your résumé, bio, video clips of your work, and possibly a blog. On your blog you can talk about your life, your interests, and what inspires you. When searching for representation, this can give your prospective agent/manager tools and personal information about you, which will enable him to pitch and represent you the best he can.

Personally, and after speaking to industry professionals, the general consensus is that five years ago websites were great, but now they are becoming somewhat of a dated concept. If you are not thinking about making a website but looking for an online media hosting site to post your demo reels or videos as an alternative, I would suggest using the most popular services: Vimeo or YouTube. If you want a more professional and private approach where you can protect your videos with passwords and share the links privately with viewers, use Vimeo or Vimeo PRO.

Any moment has the power to evoke greatness—that is, as long as we stay focused and driven toward our greatest potential and goals. These tools are part of a marketing plan and are meant to create a package for you to get your foot in the door. To get to that stage, you want to have your material in order, set definite goals, and give yourself a time frame for those goals to be achieved. This will help keep you on track and motivated.

CHAPTER THREE:

Unions

Unions are organizations that are authorized to represent employees before management and help with negotiating benefits for the employees. SAG-AFTRA is the largest actors' union that represents actors and helps to weed out the scams of some industry projects. To most people, the entertainment world for a professional actor means being a union actor. The benefit of joining the actors' union is that the union only represents legitimate projects, so it will allow you to find decent-paying jobs, as well as provide employment benefits and even insurance and retirement accounts.

HOW DO I JOIN THE UNION?

There is a bit of a catch-22 with gaining union status. You have to be union to do a union job, but you can't do a union job until you are union status. Most people become union through something called a Taft-Hartley, which allows you an opportunity to work on a union job, and the production opts you in. After you have worked on the project, you can enter the union. This is your first union job according to the federal Taft-Hartley Act, which means a non-SAG-AFTRA actor may be cast and work for a SAG-AFTRA project under a union contract for one month or thirty days, after which the actor can contact the union directly and join the union if desired.

Union contracts are called signatories and have to meet specific requirements with wages and working conditions within the union scale, which varies depending on the budget of the project. So this catch-22 is a bit of a problem, but I have found a loophole. If nobody is willing to Taft-Hartley you into their project, you can create your own project and apply for it to become a SAG- AFTRA project using their signatory agreements. You can then cast yourself as an actor in the project (so employ yourself, resulting in Taft-Hartleying yourself) into your own production. By doing this, you will be able to apply for union status. Voilà!

CAN I ONLY BELONG TO ONE UNION?

SAG-AFTRA is the biggest union, but most people who attempt to pursue a full-time performing career are usually members of SAG-AFTRA as well as other unions. Available unions include Actors Equity Association, American Film Institute, and American Guild of Musical Artists. There are no rules saying you can only be a member of only one union at any given time.

WHAT DO I DO ONCE I BECOME UNION?

Once you have your SAG-AFTRA card, make sure you sign up for the new members' orientation. Being a union member lets you sign up for a range of resources and benefits, so signing up for the orientation takes you through an introduction program and offers an explanation of everything the union has to offer. They explain everything from initiation fees and health coverage to the correct way to execute reports and contracts. They even have free workshops by casting directors who are currently casting shows. Doing workshops outside of SAG-AFTRA would normally would cost fifty to a hundred dollars, but as a member, you get them for free! If you've worked this hard to get into the union, make the most of the resources they offer you.

CHAPTER FOUR:

Visa and Immigrations

If you want to work in the States, you need a work permit. If you want to work in the States as an actor, you need what is called an O-1 working visa. Now think of this as one of the most (if not *the* most) important job application of your life to date. The O-1 visa is technically a nonimmigrant work visa that is valid for three years at a time. The visa is for "those who possess extraordinary ability in the sciences, arts, education, business, or athletics, or who have a demonstrated record of extraordinary achievement in the motion picture or television industry and have been recognized nationally or internationally for those achievements." – U.S Citizenship and Immigration Services. Url: http://www.uscis.gov/working-united-states/temporary-workers/o-1-individuals-extraordinary-ability-or-achievement/o-1-visa-individuals-extraordinary-ability-or-achievement

In order to obtain an O-1 visa, you will need to meet the following requirements:

A SPONSOR

A US-based agent, manager, or production company will need to act as the sponsor or petitioner for your visa. This is the person who will vouch to the government that his company will employ you. Although this sounds demanding, it's really very simple. Your lawyer will just send your sponsor some basic paperwork that takes about five to ten minutes to fill out. Without your sponsor, though, you have no case.

A LAWYER

You will also need an immigration lawyer. I recommend getting one who specializes in O-1 visas. There are so many immigration lawyers and thousands of visas with different guidelines. You want a lawyer who doesn't have to flip through the guideline book for a refresher. After all, you pay a lawyer to already know that. A comfort is that most good immigration lawyers will only take on cases if they think they have a high chance of getting approved, which keeps the law offices' success rate high and doesn't waste anyone's time or money.

(Also, here is some inside info: no matter what state your lawyer is in, all O-1 cases go to one of two service centers, either Vermont or California, depending on where your sponsor company is located.)

REFERENCES

You want to highlight your successes in acting. Your lawyer will go over what your case specifically needs. Each person has different experience in the industry, and some areas are stronger and more experienced for others. To back up your case, you want references, and I don't mean from your family members. You need references from as many established industry professionals as possible. You want at least fifteen, but I would recommend twenty to be secure or even more if you can get them—the more the better. You're spending time and money, so you don't want to give people any reason to say no to you. References can be from industry professionals you've worked with or who have seen you perform. Seek out actors, teachers, acting coaches, agents, directors, producers, or writers—anyone in the vein of performance who you have history with and preferably who has a reputable career.

The O-1 visa is known as the extraordinary talent visa, meaning these reference letters are to show immigration that industry professionals have witnessed your talent. The testimonials are meant to attest to how talented and deserving you are to work in America as an actor. You want the letters to include the words *extraordinary talent* as much as possible so you are identifying the content and acknowledging what you are applying for.

You might be thinking, *What if I have references but they aren't sure about what to say or have no time to write the letter?* Well, sometimes law firms will write your recommendation letters for you as part of their service, which will be reflective in their fees. If your lawyer doesn't offer this service and the people serving as your references are unsure what to include in their letters, you can take the pressure off of them by writing the letters yourself. After you have drafted a letter, simply send it to your reference for approval and signing—done deal.

PRESS

This refers to any and all press relevant to your career, including articles that have been written about you or that you have been featured in that depict or display your talent. These can be anything in the form of publicity—newspaper clippings, show reviews, magazine articles, or online features. I even included some reviews of shows I was in as a child (including the hilarious photos that accompanied them). The more press you can provide, the better. You are trying to provide evidence that you are at the top of your field, because the government is essentially considering you for this visa based on the premise that you will be an asset to the industry when you come to America. Also, if you are granted this visa, you are taking a potential job away from an American candidate, so you have to state why you deserve that opportunity more than, or as much as, an American actor with press evidence showing success stories.

MONEY

An O-1 visa isn't cheap. Including all lawyer fees, filing fees, and union letters, the total costs can range between four thousand and seven thousand dollars, depending on the lawyer you choose. This is on top of what money you will need to live off of during your first few months in Los Angeles. There isn't any way to get around paying for a lawyer when it comes to visas unless you book a US network or cable show. If that's the case, then the network or show will pay your lawyer's fees.

This could happen from your home country by submitting an audition tape and booking the role, but that is usually the only exception. Generally, this only applies if you book a lead role, because it's too much work for the network for someone who is only a costar or guest star.

If you know this is what you want to do and where you need to be, then follow your instinct (I did) and just prepare to start saving those pennies, because you're going to need a lawyer. As mentioned earlier, most good immigration lawyers won't accept a case or money for it if they don't think they can win.

During my research, I interviewed Lyz Mancini, an O-1 visa expert from David Camacho Law PLLC. David Camacho Law is a New York-based immigration firm with clients from all over the world. It is also the firm that helped me obtain my O-1.

During our interview, I asked Lyz for the main piece of advice she would give to someone considering an O-1 visa application.

> First and foremost, I would suggest to save everything. All your tear sheets, call sheets, pay stubs, articles, playbills, etc. Do not throw anything out because it is all very valuable for your petition. Also never say no to press, as articles and interviews about you are gold when the O-1 is concerned. Lastly, make sure you give yourself a good amount of time to put together the petition and to wait for the

visa to be approved. This will reduce stress and result in the most attractive and thorough petition.- Lyz Mancini (David Camacho Law PLLC) in discussion, 2013.

If you are in New York at any stage of your journey, I would suggest going to one of David Camacho Law's free monthly educational seminars designed to educate and inform the public on immigration and business matters. These seminars are a perfect opportunity to learn basic and meaningful information about the complex immigration process in a relaxed and friendly setting. Obviously, because they helped me obtain my O-1, I highly recommend them. More information can be found at their website: http://dcamacholaw.com.

You're the key decision maker because it's your career, but having a good team helping you manage your career and guiding you with decisions is essential to finding success in this industry. You're going to need representation if you want to advance your career to the next level. Before starting your search for an agent and manager, it's important to remind yourself that although these people represent you and help submit you for work, they do not guarantee you work.

Let's start by breaking down who's who and how they relate to you. That way, you have a clear understanding of who does what and how they relate to you and your career, which is always helpful). Being clear on each individual's function and purpose will help you facilitate the right team and supportive network.

It may seem strange as a creative artist, but for a moment think of yourself as a business or a product. As a product, you have a brand you are selling to the industry. Ask yourself the following questions: What is my unique selling point? What do I do better than anyone else? Am I naturally more of a leading lady or better as the nerdy sidekick?

Think about actors like Clint Eastwood, who for years portrayed characters with the tough-guy image, or Meg Ryan, who was known for playing the cute, girl-next-door characters. There are always people who will say that you shouldn't put yourself in a stereotype, but more often than not, it will help you to break into the field rather than inhibit you. Once you are established, you can challenge yourself and break through any box to explore characters with different ranges, especially because you will have some experience.

Consider what your niche market might be. Don't get me wrong; this doesn't turn into an actor walking around saying, "This is my brand." How many Oscar-winning actors do you hear of walking around talking like that? The answer is none.

Also, if you don't have representation, you probably don't know what your market, brand, or type is. It is something to think about. If you know the answer or have an idea before having your agent and manager meetings, it will help you obtain representation and also help your reps when they are considering what roles they can market and pitch you for. Your representation will be pitching you to casting directors to get you auditions, so you both need to be on the same page. They need to know what they are marketing, because they are making money off of you too. So, who's who?

AGENTS

An agent is someone who represents an actor and markets him. An agent knows her client's talents and abilities and is authorized by the actor to find, submit, and pitch him for all appropriate auditions or work opportunities that she has access to.

An agent is legally the only representative who can negotiate contracts aside from a lawyer for the actor. You may also have more than one agent; for example, agencies often have different divisions covering different categories, such as theatrical (film and television), commercial, print, and voice-over. Not all agencies cover all categories of media; only smaller agencies tend to have actors covered across the board. If they do have multiple categories, you aren't restricted to be across the board with that one agency. Most actors I know have a different agent with different agencies for each category.

Like life, most places are better at certain things than others, and with agencies, the same notion applies. Agents work on a commission basis and generally take a 10 to 15 percent cut (usually more than a manager, because they market and negotiate the deals). Unlike a manager, agents need an agent's license to operate, which is authorized by the actors' union (SAG-AFTRA) to make them a legal and legitimate agency. Because they have to have a license, you are less likely to be sucked into some scam agency. Any agent who isn't franchised by the union is one thing—not legit. And what you want to do? Run!

MANAGERS

The first distinction to be aware of is that agencies require a license, while managers do not. Because of this, you might find it is easier to obtain a manager than an agent. Keep in mind that the reasoning behind this is that anyone can be a manager, because they don't need a license. Your mum could even be your manager (just look at the Kardashians).

The major difference between a manager and agent is the word *personal*. A manager is sometimes referred to as your personal manager, because she plays a more personal role to guide, advise, and counsel you on the long-term goals of your developing career. First and foremost, you want a manager who believes in you and has time to invest in you to get you started.

A touchy subject is managers who charge a fee for their services. Some have even been known to charge their clients a monthly rate. There is no law against this, but there also isn't any law or license to filter out who becomes a manager. As a result, you find considerably more shady people offering their services and setting up little offices claiming they are managers. I would recommend staying away from these types; even some of the top managers in the world don't charge a fee. It is also not as motivating for them to work for you, because they are already getting paid. The best way to find a legitimate agent is to do your own research through the Internet, workshops, or referrals.

I interviewed one of Hollywood's top , managers Holly Lebed, who has been in the industry for more than two decades and now has her own personal management company.

Holly Lebed:

What do you look for in a client?

Longevity. I've always felt that a talent should have just one manager their entire career. Of course, it doesn't always work out this way, but for me, I look for the qualities of passion and dedication.When I want to represent a client, it's usually because I go with a gut feeling. Gut feelings can look and feel many different ways. Do they engage me? Does my gut tell me they've got 'it'? Do I have chemistry with that person? And that doesn't mean do I want to have sex with that person, but it's do they have a spark that I want to watch them in a theatre play and/or film? It's a raw, gut feeling. Also, do I think the potential client has the work ethic, and are they mentally and physically healthy enough that I can handle working with this client daily?

The client must be on the same page and have a realistic approach of themselves and what roles they are suitable for; they must display self-awareness. That way, the actor helps me to help them by not fighting what comes naturally to them. They accept their natural look, gifts, and aura, and once they have been successful in their natural box, they can break out of any given stereotype.

Also, while an agent or manager is making their assessment of you during a meeting, make sure you also evaluate them to see if you think they would be a good fit for you. Don't just accept whatever offer is on the table. Regardless, no interview is ever a waste of time—no meeting, no audition, no opportunity. However, when you start taking meetings with representation, be mindful of where that agent or manager is in their life or career. Like if they have a roster of huge moneymakers and they just don't have time for you, or perhaps they are just starting out but don't have enough connections. Some of the bigger agents may want to sign you, but if you are starting from scratch, they may not have time to facilitate your career the way it needs and not realize it. It's like ordering too much food off the menu; their eyes are bigger than their stomach.

Do you take on a client if you have an actor with a similar look in the same category?

No two talents are the same, but would I pick someone who is a clone of someone already on my roster? No. But I wouldn't say no to actors with similarities. This is different for every agent/management company. As an agent, there is more room for flexibility with clients, but being a manager, you want to have a much smaller list.

What do you consider necessary steps for a new client to do when starting out?

Network. Network. Network. Any talent, no matter how large their team, manager, agent, attorney, publicist, etc., needs to always have the mind-set that they are ultimately responsible for their own business. That actor also needs to educate themselves; enroll in acting classes, read, and research—seek intelligence. Be curious—go to every film, play, and television show currently on, so when you get weird last-minute sides, you are familiar with the style of that show so you can audition intelligently. Also, be physical; join a gym and look after yourself so you are physically and mentally healthy. An actor has to do more than just be pretty these days.

How do you suggest for clients to keep active during slow periods in the industry?

Take classes, join theatre companies, create their own work, and get involved in projects outside themselves that are of being service to others, like charity work. Generally be productive, proactive, and curious about life and your career.

Also there's a strange phenomenon we're witnessing that I feel is a result of the combined effects of a downed global economy, a shift in the taste of the viewer, and the exponential rapid increase in technology. In a nutshell, the most lucrative demographic in the entertainment industry are men and women ages eighteen to thirty-five, the children of the baby boomers, known as the millennials, or generation Y. In my opinion, due to the creation of the Internet and cell phones and by being witness to catastrophes like 9/11 and the economic collapse, a new viewer, with much different tastes and motivations, has been birthed, leading to a shift in desirable content.

A demographic once entertained by shows like *Seinfeld*, *Friends*, *M*A*S*H*, and *Cheers* now demand the content of a *Breaking Bad*, *The Sopranos*, *Mad Men*, or *Game of Thrones*. These changes in the viewers' sensibilities have created a demand on influencers to provide an ever-increasing-in-quality product. This increase of high-quality television being produced, and the steady income being on a show provides, has created an attraction to big-name talent that used to be typically reserved for film studios by highly lucrative holding and production deals that few are willing to risk now. Add on top of this the ever-increasing ability for an individual or a small team to create their own material, post it on a social or new media outlet, and become recognized almost overnight, has lead to competition for an emerging artist that we have not yet seen in any previous generation.

Today's market, for better and worse, allows talent an unprecedented ability to never have a slow period. With new media outlets such as YouTube, Vine, Facebook, Instagram, etc. becoming the new norm on distributing original content, anyone with a few friends and some decent equipment can create a product to distribute to the public and expand that person's awareness in the marketplace. Add onto creating your own material, there are endless classes, coaches, schools, and talent to never stop working for yourself and improving your skill set.

What do you think about managers who charge fees?

There are managers who charge fees? Enough said.

What is the best piece of advice someone has given you relative to the industry?

I have a few. Firstly, to thine own self be true. Second, have the ability to think fast and be flexible. If those aren't pretty inherent characteristics of your nature, I suggest you find something else to do. Third, any success in this business is an exception to the rule.

Holly has been in the business for more than thirty years, being an agent and a manager for boutique agencies and big corporations before developing her own management agency.

So here you now have a great set of advice from one of the industries highly experienced professionals. Take and absorb the advice given as much as possible then apply this to your career. Now to continue on, in addition to your agent and manager, there are other players you may want to add to your team as you become more established and start working more.

ACTING COACHES

The industry is a business, and you're an artist, so how do you keep that sense of play in your work when you are organizing the logistics? This is where an acting coach is one of the most valuable tools you can have. Acting is, more than anything, a creative form of expression, which is a craft. So many actors get lost in the logistics of the industry and forget what it's essentially about—acting. Even the best actors in Hollywood understand the importance of constantly improving their craft no matter how far they've come. Having an acting coach helps you practice your craft, and coaches can also often act as creative mentors. A lot of actors who are successful in Hollywood aren't necessarily the best actors, but they find a good balance between the business and their passion for the craft.

There are hundreds of group acting classes to help keep you fresh and refine your skills. If you are already a working actor, you can opt for private sessions with an acting coach and work on specific material and discuss goals. Now, choosing the right acting coach is crucial, because not every teacher is right for every actor. Just because a coach worked for someone else, doesn't mean he will work for you. I would recommend auditing an acting class first. Most acting coaches or studios offer free audits before committing so you can feel out if their method is right for you.

In Los Angeles, you can have your pick, because there are coaches for just about everything— improv, scene study, audition technique, comedy, on-camera classes, you name it, it's out there. So enjoy the process and shop around until you feel comfortable with someone who is good match for you.

PUBLICISTS

You will not need a publicist until you have a few high-profile bookings behind you, which is generally a good thing, because publicists can be expensive. If you book a network show or film, the show will typically have its own publicist so you will get publicity already paid for. Only if you hire a personal publicist will you have to pay three thousand to five thousand dollars a month for their services. Their job is to create a buzz about you by promoting you and the work you have done. Usually, your publicist operates by getting you exposure with interviews and invites for industry events like, screenings, mixers, or red carpet events. I wouldn't worry too much about finding a publicist at this stage. When you are at that stage, your agent or manager should have connections to point you in the right direction.

ENTERTAINMENT LAWYERS

Your agent will negotiate your contracts, but when dealing with the bigger deals, some agents may not feel comfortable with the finer points of multipage contracts. For this reason, it's good to have an entertainment lawyer as your career grows. There are specific lawyers who deal with entertainment contracts; your agency may even have an entertainment lawyer they already work in conjunction with, which will save you the time and effort to find out your own. They will also already have a relationship established with them, so the transition of having them part of your team is even smoother.

Aside from your team, there are many industry professionals that we could talk about, but to get a better understanding of how the industry operates, there are two specific heavyweights you need to know about that relate to you as an actor: casting directors and producers.

CASTING DIRECTORS

A casting director is someone who is hired by a network or film production company to cast the project on offer and find the best person for the job.

It is your agent's or manager's job to get you the interview or audition, but the casting director is the person who will make or break if you step forward to be seen by the producers at the final stages of the casting process. In those final stages, the casting director brings her favorite options (usually about three to five actors) to perform in front of the producers.

PRODUCERS

Producers have many roles from developing and creating the concept to executive producers who help facilitate finding the funding for the project. In this case, producers are key in deciding who gets the role, unless it's a network television series. In that case, the network would also decide along with the producers whether to give you the job. It is a process of many approvals;

you go through the casting director, who then sends her picks to the producers, and the producers then decide who they like best and is most suited for the part. If the network or whoever is airing the show approves, then, voilà, you have booked a job!

I never realized how true it is until I moved to Hollywood that, yes, becoming a famous movie star is a dream that inspires most, but in reality, most stars are products that are strategically created and facilitated by a team of skilled professionals. These people spend hours focused on creating, developing, honing, and publicizing the maximum potential of an individual. So if you want a chance to become one of Hollywood's elite, you need to have patience and pleasant persistence to build your foundation from the ground up.

Seriously, it won't happen overnight, although that's a nice idea. You need to take control and start with the little things, like perfecting the skills of your craft with class and student projects and then establishing the right team of representation. It's often tempting to take the shortcut, the first person who offers you representation, or the cheaper option in classes or photographs, but think of your career's longevity. Imagine it's a house; you can try to build a house solidly so you have something of value and quality, or you can take the shortcut and build it cheaply and quickly. I'm pretty sure we know how long it will last.

> *Passion for something is just not enough. You need to put your time in on the core skills—there's no way around it.*
>
> —Quincy Jones, twenty-seven-time Grammy award winner and seventy-nine-time Grammy nominated American record producer, conductor, arranger, composer, television producer, and trumpeter

CHAPTER SIX:

Having a Plan

It's time to facilitate your action plan for success! You know what actors' tools you need and who you need to have on your team, but where do you start, and how do you put it all together?

A MAIL-OUT

In chapter two, we got your acting tools organized. Now you have a nice little package with all your material about you, and we want to get you some interviews with agents and managers to set up your team. You should collect the information of good agencies or management companies you respect, have researched, or have been referred to and do what is called a mail-out. A mail-out is when you mail your acting package—your photograph, résumé, and reel, accompanied by a cover letter—to the representatives you want to set up meetings with. Make sure you mail your package in an envelope large enough to ensure you don't crease or fold your material. It doesn't create a good first impression when they open the envelope and have to untangle your headshot and résumé just to see what you look like.

FOLLOW-UP

People in the business get busy, and even if they are interested, they might forget to call you back. If you sent a mail-out to a person, make sure you follow up with a phone call to his office. The best time to call is a week later so you are still fresh in his mind, but two weeks is also sufficient. Also, if you have already met with representation or been to a casting director workshop, send the person you met with a handwritten thank-you note. Never underestimate the power of a handwritten thank-you note, especially because so many things are currently electronic that we are slowly losing touch with each other. Sometimes the simplest means of communication after meeting someone are the most valued.

However, if you haven't met with casting or reps and are following up after a mail-out, you should call to follow up. When you call, you'll most often get an assistant or secretary who will ask you to leave a message. Just leave your name and number and mention that you sent some material over. Be sure to request that the person you are trying to reach give you a call when he has a moment. Don't be discouraged by the secretary not putting you straight through; this is standard and is how agencies filter their calls. It's also possible that the person is in the middle of something, but if a rep is interested, he will call you back. If you don't hear from him, he likely isn't interested.

A rejection can happen for many reasons. I have found that usually it's because you might not have enough credits or you're not a member of the union. It may be as simple as the person might already be representing someone similar to you. In this case, it's not usually in a person's interest to represent multiple actors of the same type. The more variety of actors he has on his books, the more jobs he can send people out for, and the greater the chance that he will make money.

Don't take rejection personally. In this business, persistence is key, and things change quickly. You may do a mail-out the following year and discover a client has have left that same person, so he now has room for new clients and will call you back. Just keep at it and submit to as many reputable agents and managers as possible.

WORKSHOPS

I decided to speak to Scott David, top Hollywood casting director of CBS's hit television show *Criminal Minds* and long-standing member of the Casting Society of America. The transcript of the interview follows:

> *You're considered one of Hollywood's top casting directors and have been in the business more than two decades. What's your opinion on casting director workshops and agent/manager showcases?*

> Casting director workshops are the most valuable marketing tool for new actors, seasoned actors, and veteran actors to showcase themselves, to network and link themselves with industry professionals. The prolific nature of acting workshop studios as a learning experience is unparalleled. The actors get firsthand information directly from the industry professional and can then utilize this information when opportunities arise for them in the acting world. Creating these relationships is crucial in the actor's developmental stage of their career. Agent manager showcases allow the actors to demonstrate their abilities and to market themselves to see if the industry warms up to them in a live, one-on-one manner. This opportunity for new actors to actually meet with reps once again is invaluable, and all actors should take the time out to learn how to act and react to an agent or a manager, which is somewhat different than working in front of a casting professional.

How often do you bring actors in for auditions who you have met through workshops?

Workshops are a learning experience for the actors and the industry professional. Both parties learn things about another; there is no expectation or pressures of auditions that might come into the scenario.

So from a top industry casting director's view, they're invaluable, and to make things even easier, they're very accessible! Workshops are held all around the city by a number of independent companies that charge a one-time fee for you to attend. So we know workshops are a great investment in our careers, but what happens apart from meeting the casting director or agent/manager representative? Following are some things to consider in your search.

WHAT'S THE FORMAT OF A WORKSHOP?

Often, workshops start with a question-and-answer session, so this is also a great way to ask any industry-related questions that you're curious about and want clarified. Make sure you think about your questions carefully, though, because you don't want to make yourself look stupid. Like Scott David said, "Both parties learn things about one another." Because of this, you don't want them to learn the wrong things!

After the Q&A, each person gets the chance to perform a piece of material, either a monologue or a scene. You can pick the material yourself, or it will be given to you on the night of the workshop. Having the chance to perform in front of these industry professionals is essentially what you pay to go to the workshops for, so put some time and effort in your material, especially if you're performing your own work.

HOW LONG ARE MOST WORKSHOPS?

In terms of the length, most often the whole event can last anywhere from one to four hours, depending on the number of people attending and the length of the material by those performing. If they have more people signed up for the session, they will have a time limit for the material, but it's generally two minutes.

HOW MUCH ARE THEY?

Most workshops vary in price, depending on the company and casting director or showcase, but usually range from thirty to ninety dollars. You can go nuts and book every workshop in town if you have the finances, but I would suggest you do your research and find out who is casting what shows, projects you might be suitable for, or agents you think are accessible to you with the credits you have and who you want really want to meet.

HOW DO I KNOW WHICH ONES TO GO TO?

Think of workshops like a great way to get your foot in the door and perform and meet agents and/or managers you want to represent you or casting directors you want to audition for in order to be booked for the shows they're casting. For an agent/manager showcase, ask yourself what agencies or managers you want to meet and who you think would be the best fit for your team. Also consider whether you're looking for theatrical or commercial representation.

When considering which casting director workshops to attend, find out who's currently casting shows that you suit. Consider whether you want to be cast on prime-time drama, comedy, or feature films, and then look up the casting directors' credits online at IMDB.com (International Movie Database) to see what or if they're currently casting. It's no use paying all that money to go to a workshop with a casting director who's retired or hasn't cast a show in ten years. The chances of such a person bringing you in for an audition or hiring you probably aren't very high.

INTERVIEWS

According to Holly Lebed,

Actors need to drop the word *brand* from their vocabulary. Know it, acknowledge it, but if you're meeting with an agent or manager, you don't have a brand. You should know what you're marketable as, and the smart actor knows how to answer that question but knows that it is not the conversation point for an actor. Branding is not the conversation of a true creative or how a real actor talks. If you're using that language when you walk into the room with an agent/manager meeting, it will most likely repel them. Their job is to market you; your job is to be the best version of *yourself* and know who you are.

Let's go through the interview process and prepare you for your interview. Just approach the interview in exactly the same way you would a job interview. When you meet with casting directors and representation, you want to be yourself. If you're not normally the friendliest person just try to be as warm, friendly, and relaxed as possible so you can leave a positive lasting impression.

WHAT DO I WEAR?

Dress well and comfortably and apply the same criteria you did when you had your headshot taken. It's usually best to wear clothes that make you look natural and versatile for different roles, because an agent will be thinking about how she could market you from the moment you step through the door. So don't worry; there's no need to dress up like you're off to the Oscar's. It's also important to remember to go easy on the heavy makeup. Keep everything natural, neat, and casual.

BEING ON TIME?

The second biggest pointer I can give is to be on time! If you're late, that tells the agent you're not reliable or serious about your career. If this is a job interview and you're late, then you're giving yourself a disadvantage before you even arrive. I had an acting teacher when I was growing up who always said, "If you're not early, you're late." It's stuck with me my entire life, like that little voice in the back of your head that won't shut up. In this case, it's probably the best little voice that could be stuck parroting information. Try aiming to arrive twenty minutes early to prevent any mishaps that could occur, because this is LA and the traffic is horrific. Plus, being Hollywood, you never know what could happen (in a horrifying and exciting way).

WHAT TO BRING?

Bring at least two copies of your headshot and résumé. If you have multiple headshots with different looks, bring those too so representation can see all the possibilities they could submit you for. Despite what you think, when most agents look at you, they are thinking about marketing you and how marketing you can translate to dollar signs. Ultimately, they don't make money unless you do.

Upon arrival, you want everything you have brought with you stapled and organized, ready to present. It doesn't look good if you have to pull it out and organize it on the table when you're asked for it. Just be professional. You worked so hard to get this interview to start with, so make the most of it.

If this is a theatrical representation interview and you have a demo reel, you can also bring that with you on a disc. That way, the agent can also see examples of how you translate on screen. Be prepared to leave your demo reel with the agent if asked. A disc is usually the cheapest and best way to do that.

WHAT QUESTIONS SHOULD I ASK IN THE INTERVIEW?

You're looking for a partner, so you want an agent you have a good relationship with—chemistry. Some agents aren't always good at interviewing clients, so help them out by being relaxed and easygoing. Describe to them your career, your desires, your commitment, your training, what you feel you can do, and what you are prepared to sacrifice. Whatever questions the agent asks you, always answer truthfully, regardless of what you think he would like to hear. You need to be truthful so he can properly assess whether to take you on as a client. If the agent ends up representing you, you need to trust each other completely. The agent will need to know exactly where you're at with your career so he can help get you to the next level.

Lastly, aim to go in and have a good time. If you've said everything you want to say, then leave it at that. Some people don't know when to stop talking, and that's as bad as being silent and as boring as a piece of wood. The agent ultimately wants to get to know you, so go in and chat with him. This will give the agent a general feeling about you and make it a fun experience for you. No matter what happens with each interview, use it as an experience to learn and grow. You have nothing to lose. You didn't have this person as representation before your interview, so you haven't lost anything. You've only gained more knowledge and power.

GOAL SETTING

There truly is no growth without an action plan, and goals help give you stepping stones to success by breaking down tasks that seem light-years away. To get you climbing on that success ladder, it's all about establishing goals that drive you to your highest potential and increase your chances of success. Think about goals as a daily habit you want to introduce into your plan and one to frequently monitor so you're revising your goals as you go along to see that you remain on course. There's no question of the direct correlation between success and the simple act of writing your goals down on paper.

You want to make goal setting a habit, because there are even studies that show writing your goals down on paper gets the wheels of success spinning. When making your goals, you want to create clear and specific goals that are realistic.

For example, here is a nonrealistic goal: "Tomorrow I will be the biggest movie star in Hollywood." Although it sounds nice, it's not the most practical goal. Start by making short-term, midterm, and long-term goals in the form of daily, weekly, monthly, and yearly items. Again, breaking your goals down so specifically will help remind you about your purpose and keep you on track and focused.

It may sound like a lot of work, but in reality, it will help simplify things. Think of it like planning a drive from one side of the country to the other, as if you're drawing out a map on how to get there. On the map you want to mark all the places you want to stop along the way; you want to get gas or food and not get stuck in the middle of nowhere. The same is true for your career. Maybe you don't drive across the country every day, but I'm sure you've made a to-do list. No matter how big or small, it's the same concept.

You can start breaking things down by asking yourself a few questions: Where am I now? Where do I want to be? And how do I plan to get there?

Here's a formula for breaking down your goals into various categories:

Yearly goals. Create an overview of things you want to achieve during the next year. Then prioritize this list in order of what you want to achieve most, making clear, concise goals. You can filter the goals that aren't major prioritizes around your bigger goals and then break this down further by what you want to achieve during each of the next twelve months.

Monthly goals. From your yearly goal layout, you may already have some monthly goals. Even so, at the beginning of each month, you should write down your goals for that month and prioritize those things you want to get done. You might need to filter or add specific goals.

Weekly goals. At the start of each week, write your goals for the next seven days. You can block them out for what you want to achieve each day or create a broad overview of the week. Either way, be realistic about what you can achieve in this time.

Daily goals. This will look like a daily to-do list. Step by step, you've broken down your most important goals. Now we're getting into the tiny steps and dividing the goals into even smaller steps of daily goals. This way, each day you are making a step toward your bigger plans that you have laid out in your monthly and yearly goals.

Keep your goals close and refer to them regularly, which will keep them in clear focus. As you reflect back over the day, week, month, and year, you will be surprised at the progress you have made toward achieving your annual goals. Just be aware that as you write your goals, it's important you realize you can't have it all at once.

It's hard to succeed if you spread yourself too thin and become scattered, so prioritize your list of goals and be reasonable about what can be accomplished in a block of time. There are no shortcuts to greatness. It comes through consistent effort with the little things you do each day that build your career step by step. If you're not doing something on a regular basis to make your dream a reality, then maybe you don't really want the dream. That may be hard to hear, but why else wouldn't you be willing to do whatever it takes to achieve it. Seriously, if you really want something, then there shouldn't be any excuses. There is always time to do the things that are really important to you.

I want to be a great actor someday, and I've decided there's no use philosophizing; the only way is to work at my craft.

—Al Pacino, Oscar-, Academy-, and Golden Globe-winning and nominated actor

Even the most famous actors in the world train and have acting coaches on set, because they know that as you start to evolve as a person, so does your work. Once you start this process of developing the specifics of your craft and making new discoveries, it's a lifelong process, which is great because you can never be too good or too knowledgeable at what you do. The fastest way to start this process of becoming a more seasoned actor is taking regular classes and auditioning. Being in ongoing classes is a key stepping stone to success in this business, and it helps you grow and keeps you sharp for your next major audition.

You could also look at your move to Hollywood as an opportunity to tune up and fall in love with your craft all over again. You should try to take a variety of acting classes with different styles to make you the most well-rounded actor possible. This also gives you an advantage over other actors, because by studying, you're increasing and honing your skill set. Having more skills gives you an advantage over your competition. So try to take as many classes as possible—everything from comedy classes to audition technique classes. If you're new to Hollywood, it's also great to have some respected and recognizable acting coaches on your résumé. If you don't have many solid credits, this can also give casting directors and representation a good association for what your performance level is like by who you've trained with.

Now you just have to find good classes. There are many resources to help you find a good match, with the Internet, word-of-mouth suggestions, or referrals usually being the best way. There are lots of classes in Los Angeles to choose from, and not every acting coach will be right for every person.

I suggest that when you're approaching the search for a new acting teacher, think of the process like you're looking for a new partner to add to your actor's tool kit. It's as if you're going shopping, and you want to shop around to find the best fit. The best way to do this is by taking free class audits. Audits are when you can sit and watch the class for free without participating.

There are some clear red flags you want to keep an eye out for when auditing:

1) Teachers who don't critique.
2) Condescending teachers.
3) Teachers who indulge in bringing up actors' painful history.
4) Overcrowded classes with so many students the teacher doesn't even know the students' names.

To help start you off with your research and point you in the direction of some potential classes to audit, look at some of the coaches below. All are respected and reputable Acting coaches in Los Angeles with different styles and approaches.

ACTING COACHES AND SCHOOLS

Anthony Meindl
Ivana Chubbuck
Larry Moss
Margie Harber
Howard Fine
Bernard Hiller
Carter Thor
Diana Castle
Playhouse West
Beverly Hills Playhouse
Stella Adler
The Ruskin Group Theatre

COMEDY AND IMPROV TRAINING

The Groundlings Theatre
The Upright Citizens Brigade
Second City

VOCAL TRAINING

Denise Woods (dialects)
The Voice Box LA (singing)

AUDITION COACHING

Amy Jo Berman
Saxon Trainor
Craig Wallace

I spoke to Head Casting Director Scott David and Writer/Director Katt Shea about their views and advice on actors moving to Los Angeles and enrolling in acting classes.

The following advice came from Scott David, head casting director of *Criminal Minds* at CBS and A&E, CSA member, and owner of The Actors Link:

> Have the desire to be in acting class; enroll in at least one ongoing acting class a month or two if your budget can afford it, meaning, being in class at least two to four times per week for months on end. Have a budget saved, so when you're ready and skilled enough, you can network and link yourself to casting workshops, taking anywhere from five to ten classes per month to get to know the industry professionals. You can never be too good in this industry. – Scott David (casting director of CBS show *Criminal Minds*) in discussion, 2013.

This next advice came from Katt Shea, writer, director, and creator of the cult classic film *Poison Ivy*:

> Get into a class that supports you and makes you feel good, makes you better as an actor, not one that tears you down. It's important to *build* on what does work, not constantly focus on and criticize what doesn't. If you are focused on what doesn't work, you will never get better. As a writer/director, I can give actors some very important information related to performing. In a script, the writer is writing so that the *reader* understands what's happening in the scene and to the character, but as *script* writers, we cannot get internal the way a novelist can. We have to describe what is happening visually. For example, we cannot say, "She feels deeply saddened." We have to say, "Tears run down her face," or "Her chin

trembles." So tears or trembling are simply shorthand to say someone is extremely vulnerable. It is the *actor's* job to bring the words on the page to life.

In life, people try very hard not to cry or tremble; only actors try to cry. So my advice is ignore that kind of description and *trust yourself* to bring the character to life through *your own* unique instrument by truly being in the moment living it for the very first time, not *acting* it. I ask actors, "Do you have to rehearse how you're going to feel in life?" If you are truly present, living in the moment, you shouldn't have to act at all. You will simply loan your body, emotion, heart, and soul to a character who is only words on a page. You do that by getting out of your head. That's why actors make the kind of money they do. So find an acting teacher that helps you get out of your head and off the page and live the life of the character. – Katt Shea (writer/director, creator of cult classic *Poison Ivy*) in discussion, 2013.

If you're having trouble factoring classes into your budget right now, then don't worry. You can still audit and find one that's right for you. Some have waiting lists, so you may be able to afford them by the time the class has room for you anyway. In the meantime, don't disregard unpaid acting projects as training. Student projects and other unpaid acting work that you can self-submit online give you the experience to build your résumé while practicing your craft, so they are a great opportunity to get experience. You also want to build up your résumé with as many projects and classes as possible. You don't necessarily want a résumé with a hundred student films, but it's a start for you to have some experience so you can have some material before you walk through that casting director's or agent's office door.

Student projects are also a good way to meet people. Student films usually have cast and crew who are trying to get started in the same field as you, so it can be a great way to connect and establish relationships with others for creating more projects. Ultimately, you want to create exposure for yourself and get out there, collaborate, and gain as much experience as you can. Acting by definition is actively doing something, so start creating.

In my opinion, regardless of whether you are in acting classes, you should always be actively trying to create your own projects. Actors are storytellers, and storytellers aren't restricted to telling others people's stories. The options to choose from for creating your own stories and projects are limitless; tons of actors these days have gotten huge projects from humble beginnings like a web series on YouTube.

On that note, there are also actors who have become famous for much less, so be thoughtful about which projects you give your attention to and create projects that will serve you. Don't just go and create porn because you want to create something. Think about what characters or ventures you would like to engage in that utilize your talent and then create projects that carry exposure opportunities, such as putting on a live sketch comedy performance or a play, making a short or feature film, or creating a web series. Primarily aim to get together with other artists to create projects to keep working. This way, you can possibly explore outside of your avenue as an actor and maybe try your hand at writing or directing. This helps keep you pro-active during slow periods in the industry. It also helps maintain you as a mentally healthy actor because you are being active and engaged in your career instead of sitting at home waiting for that audition e-mail or that phone to ring.

I asked Sarah Moshman, production company owner, reality television producer, and Emmy Award-winning filmmaker, if she considered it important for actors to create their own work. Her response is as follows:

> I think it's very important for actors to create their own projects. Acting is like a muscle you need to continue to exercise to improve, and if you are going on auditions and not booking any jobs, it might be that the casting directors, or your managers and agents, don't know what you are capable of. Maybe you don't even know what you're capable of yet.
>
> Get with some aspiring filmmakers and offer to star in their movie, or gather up a crew of your own and make a short piece to put up online to show what you can do. Take improv classes, or write a play and perform it. There are so many creative people around with the equipment and the talent that need you just as much as you need them. You need a solid reel or piece to exemplify your skills and your range, and if that doesn't happen organically through auditioning, you have to take matters in to your own hands. It's also a great way to learn and grow as an artist.
>
> Do your own projects, get creating by yourself or with others, then start putting it out there. Also, it helps you knowing yourself and what you want, and that is huge in any industry but especially in this one. Creating your own projects helps keep you on your path, because also you can get swept away in projects or shows when they do come up that you don't feel any passion for simply because

it's work or the pay is decent. And before you know it, you are nowhere near the path that you had originally hoped to be on. Say your dreams out loud, and never lose sight of your goals. – Sarah Moshman (Heartfelt Productions and Emmy-award winning film-maker) in discussion, 2013.

This lady is an Emmy Award-winning documentary filmmaker because she started by creating her own films, so it's safe to say her advice is pretty valid. Like all great things, your course to success is dictated by what you put in. It won't usually magically happen overnight, so keep using the tools listed in these pages and now add to that an edge by creating your own opportunities.

Above all, when embarking on the journey of creating your own content, aim to create projects of quality. Through aiming to achieve works of quality, you are generally striving for your best, which is (hopefully) what you want to show to the world. If you put out your best, that is all you can ask for, and you can walk away with satisfaction. I know a lot of artists (and not solely actors either—photographers, directors, but often most people in an artistic medium) who are ashamed of their work. Because they are the worst critics of themselves, they scare themselves out of developing new ideas. It is not our business to determine how good our work is or how valuable it is to others. Like most things in the world, people have different opinions, and each person will decide for himself.

Remain open and be aware of what directly motivates you in your work. Remember that there is a vitality and life force that is translated through you into an action. There is only one of you at this moment in time who has the skills you have, has your sense of self, and is creating this unique expression.

We are what we repeatedly do. Excellence, then, is not an act, but a habit.

—Aristotle, ancient Greek philosopher

Auditions are when actors show the casting directors and producers what they can do. Your agent or manager typically gets auditions through submitting you for a breakdown. A breakdown is like a job posting that is created by casting directors when they are about to start work on a new project. This is a listing of the project and what characters are needed, along with descriptions. Your agent or manager can then submit your information along with your headshot. If the casting director is interested, he will contact your agent and request to see you for an audition.

Auditioning requires confidence, trust, acceptance, and knowledge. Actors often find the audition process unnerving or intimidating, oftentimes working so hard for the opportunity to audition and then not even considering the work on the actual audition itself. It's normal to get nervous, but a lot of actors then develop hang-ups about the process and have certain perceptions and pressures about the situation that are entirely their own manifestations. Yes, actors can face a lot of rejection on a daily basis through auditioning, and of course, being in a medium where you are judged on your looks and have your skills constantly tested can create anxieties about certain situations. So let's stop here and bring it back to basics, remembering that you are not going to be right for every project. It is (or should be) expected that you will sometimes receive disheartening responses, but they should never be taken personally. Remind yourself in an audition room that everyone wants the actor to succeed. You want the job, and casting wants to find the right person. Everyone wants the same thing—for you to be the best person for the job. It's a well-known fact that the only way to succeed is by being relaxed at your audition and feeling out the moment—not trying to be perfect. If you are in the present moment, you are free to give your best interpretation of the character required.

The actor's job is finding work. The fringe benefit of our work is you get to act.

—Samuel L. Jackson, actor

Auditioning is a skill, and like any skill, if you want to be a professional, you need to master it. Personally, I think that the hardest step is auditioning itself. Once you have the role, it's yours to explore and play with, but you have to gain the trust of the casting directors and producers first. To get casting to have faith in your abilities, you need to employ confidence, trust, and knowledge in yourself as an actor—yes, that's easier said than done. Naturally, we are only human, and everyone has his or her moments, but practice makes perfect. In this case, auditioning isn't any different.

So yes, auditioning is nerve-racking and you might get nervous, so let's find some ways to fix this. First, the word: *auditioning*. The word itself isn't even inviting; it sounds like work. It's easy to wonder, *How am I going to impress them? How am I going to stand out?* It sounds like a burden. The definition of the word *audition* indicates the actor is on trial, and that subconsciously adds pressure to the situation, which can result in nervousness.

> Definition of Audition: A trial performance, as by an actor, dancer, or musician, to demonstrate suitability or skill.

Just like life, it's all how you look at it. Auditioning and suggesting you're on trial isn't constructive or a positive approach when you're about to demonstrate your skills in front of strangers. So start thinking about them differently and begin to call your auditions *opportunities*. You're there to succeed, and to do that, you need to be relaxed. An opportunity is exactly what an audition is anyhow. Using this terminology can help relax your mind and ease the pressure so you don't feel like you're on trial.

I'd also recommend starting a journal called an opportunity log where you note all the roles you've been called in for. Write down all the basic information relative to the project, such as project name, director, character, age range, location of casting, and production company. This information is great to review over time so you can uncover any patterns. What roles are you being called out for? How do people perceive you? Have things changed recently, like your age range or character types?

It's great to reflect on what parts you go out for, and you can use this as a guide to revise and track your progress during your career. Because you constantly grow and change, so will your work. Now there are some key elements to auditions that will be outlined below to help simplify the audition process so there are no surprises on the day.

PREPARATION, SIDES, AND COLD READING

If you're failing to plan, you're planning to fail.

—Winston Churchill, prime minister, politician, and Nobel Prize winner of Literature

Preparation for your auditions is essential. You really need to invest the time. Do as much preparation as you can before you go into your audition. Know your role before you go in; do research about the project and your character. For example, if the show your auditioning for is currently on television, be sure to watch it. Knowledge is power, especially in the audition room.

Before the audition you will be given what are called sides, which are specific scenes or a few pages out of the complete script for you to show your interpretation of the character. Oftentimes, the sides will be sent to you by your agent via e-mail or posted online so you will have them before your audition. (The most common outlet for posting sides in a website called Showfax.)

The more research you do about a show, the more the sides will make sense to you. You will be able to get a better understanding of what is happening in the scene and the relationships between the characters. Once you have an understanding of the text, make yourself familiar with the sides; ideally, you should have them memorized. Always take your sides with you into the audition room even if you don't need them. You want to take your sides with you for the peace of mind of the casting director (and hopefully you too). This way, if you do so happen to forget a line from a scene, you will have the script handy, which will save the casting director from having to search for a copy. What a nightmare that would be! (It's happened to me before. Trust me, it *is* a nightmare.)

If you didn't get your sides before your audition, then you will most likely be asked to do what is called a cold read. This is when you are handed your sides at the audition; hence, they are cold, or never seen before. Casting will typically give you time to look over the lines, usually five to ten minutes, before you go in and deliver your performance. In most cases, you will be able to take the sides in with you for reference. You should try to retain as much as possible, but you have your sides to refer to if needed. Ultimately, you should aim to connect with the material and have a good understanding of your character instead of trying to be word perfect.

Cold reading is a skill, like auditioning, that becomes easier with practice. I know actors who practice cold reading and can be given a script and have all six pages memorized in ten minutes. You might wonder why casting would want you to cold read instead of having you prepare your audition. It's usually because casting is looking for a raw, fresh reading that isn't over-thought and is straight off the top of the actor's head. (Or in a worst-case scenario, it's because the script has been changed multiple times by production at the last minute.)

If casting is having you cold read the material make sure you note it is usually because prepared readings can sometimes come across too calculated and overanalyzed. As a result, they often end up looking like an over-rehearsed performance (in some cases, they actually are). If this doesn't show up in the first read, then it usually comes out when the casting director offers the actor notes or direction and the performance is too fixed for the actor to be able to smoothly adjust.

If you are expected to cold read for an audition, think about prepping outside the room as connecting to the material and aim to relax without being fixated on the words. Then, when you enter the room, keep your script away from your face and focus less on the words and more on the character's intentions. Listen and react to the person reading with you and be creative and receptive to new ideas. Above all, just play with it and have fun.

I asked veteran Hollywood Casting Director Marilyn Mandel about her thoughts on auditioning. Following is a transcript of our conversation.

> *What do you look for during the audition process?*
>
> Authenticity and truth. Acting is truth, and there is nothing more boring than an actor who has fabricated or manipulated a product. The best actors are ones who bring themselves into a character and then make strong, informed choices.
>
> *What are the key mistakes you've found actors make when auditioning?*
>
> Coming into the audition room with a performance that is final and conclusive is dull and deadly. The life happens when an actor takes risks. No one is supposed to put those pieces together, but it is absolutely so.
>
> *What would you consider the fundamentals of a good audition?*
>
> The elements of good auditions are truth and authenticity and an actor who has prepared well.
>
> Actors must fully understand the text, and this takes time and attention. Then

they can give the words a world of their own and by knowing what the subtext is about.

In your opinion what separates a good audition from a great audition?

A great audition for me would be one where I would be so drawn into the experience; I'd forget I was watching an audition. (This happens rarely.) The idea of "talent" in this industry is so overstated. That won't take you very far. The actors who create extraordinary auditions and work in general pour themselves into the work and do whatever is necessary to find the truth of the situation, the character, and the project.

What is the best piece of advice someone has given you relative to the industry?

There are no hard and fast rules in his business. But acting is not a science; it's an art. So while rules must be broken, you need to know and follow them first.

Now that some of the key fundamentals of auditioning have been covered, let's talk about audition etiquette. It's the unwritten laws of being on time, owning the room, and crashing auditions.

BEING ON TIME

This is pretty self-explanatory, really. Just be on time. I can't stress this enough, because it's the same as a job interview. An audition is a job opportunity. When you arrive on time, you show casting that you're responsible and take your work seriously. If you arrive late, you show casting that you have bad time management and are starting your first interaction by demonstrating that you don't have professional behavior. It sounds serious because it is; in production, time is money. (Heck, in most industries, time is money.) Don't waste your own or other people's time and conduct yourself in a professional manner.

Also if you're not showing professional behavior now and you haven't even booked the job yet, then when would you show professional behavior? See my point? You're not giving casting any reason to believe you would be reliable in a professional environment. If you can't be on time to the audition, what's the guarantee you wouldn't also be late to set? You then become too much of a risk. Acting is one of the most competitive industries in the world, and in Tinseltown, it's even more important to be on time.

OWNING THE ROOM

When you walk in the room, you want to walk in with ease and confidence. Walk in like you own it, like you've been there a million times before. Make sure you acknowledge the difference between owning the room with confidence and arrogance, because lots of actors get this mixed up.

Confident and arrogant are very different. A confident person is happy within himself and feels competent from the inside out. An arrogant person is ego driven and seeks external validation, usually by making others feel small and putting them down. You want to aim to create a warm, positive energy when you enter by being relaxed, easygoing, and confident.

There's nothing worse than being an arrogant actor, walking into a room, and pretending you know more than the casting director. I feel like we have all come across someone like this in our lives, so you know what I mean. If this is something you think you might be guilty of, just remember that nobody likes a know-it-all.

If I am really nervous going into castings and can't seem to focus, I like to imagine I get along with everyone and also remind myself that the audition isn't about me. As soon as I enter the room, I aim to be in character, so if anything, I'm there to give other people an experience of escapism—escapism by offering a glimpse into my interpretation of the character's slice of life. The goal is to ultimately (or hopefully) have them forget they are watching an audition. It also helps turn auditioning into a selfless act. In this instance, you're doing it for the enjoyment of others. As an added bonus, this mentally also allows you to have a sense of ease and confidence in what you are manifested as a supportive space. Please don't think because you are imagining you get along with everyone in the room that you should walk in and talk their heads off. This is simply an aim for you to have a sense of ease in your mind.

Logistically, make sure you have your material ready to give to casting as soon as you enter; your headshot and résumé should be stapled and handed over. If the casting director or assistants offer to shake your hand, make sure you have a nice, firm handshake in response. Nothing says insecure and uncertain more than a weak, limp handshake. Once you're done, don't hang about—smile, be polite, thank them, and be on your way. You're not waiting for validation, so let your performance speak for itself.

CRASHING AN AUDITION

This is a sensitive subject. The majority of the time, this is a no-no. I've heard some stories of actors who have seen a breakdown for an audition they thought they were right for and then their agent couldn't get them in, so they crashed the audition. I wouldn't advise this, but if you are going to crash an audition, you want to do it as appropriately as possible. When you go into the office, be polite. Hand your headshot and résumé to the assistant and then ask to be seen simply because you think your right for the role. There is no need to get into a song and dance about it.

Never sign in and pretend you have an audition. The assistant will take your material to the casting director. If the casting assistant or director thinks your right for the role, she will usually see you. If not, she will say no. It's that simple. If that's the case, then leave it at that and walk away.

SELF-SUBMITTING

Online submitting for breakdowns is the biggest tool for getting auditions in today's society. Your reps submit you for breakdowns online, and you want to be proactive and submit yourself too. People who get noticed in this industry are actors getting exposure by taking their careers into their own hands by creating their own work and submitting themselves for breakdowns online.

There are so many websites that offer online casting calls. They usually work on a membership basis and allow you to upload headshots, a résumé, reel, and links, for example, to your IMDB page. Each website has various differences in pricing, with some charging more per headshot or for you to add a reel to your profile. Use your discretion with this; you can spend a fortune adding demo reels and twenty headshots, none of which will actually serve you well.

You want your résumé to be current. Keep it simple by adding three key headshots—your comedy theatrical (smiling or goofy), your dramatic theatrical (more serious), and your commercial shot. If you have a reel, you can upload that too, but if you don't have one, don't worry. These websites are designed to get you work to build up your material, so it won't be long before you get enough work to create a reel.

These websites have every kind of casting call imaginable, from student films, music videos, commercials, films, web series, pilots, theatre, and everything in between. They also have union and nonunion jobs, so these casting calls can be a great way to get your SAG-AFTRA card.

Don't feel burdened by thinking you have to troll through hundreds of breakdowns from multiple websites every day. When you sign up and create your profile, you can specify exactly what type of jobs you want to be notified of, the website will send you a direct e-mail update when those breakdowns come through.

Following is a list of websites I would recommend registering for:

Actors Access, http://www.actorsaccess.com
La Casting, http://www.lacasting.com
Now Casting, http://www.nowcasting.com
CAZT, http://www.cazt.com
Casting Frontier, http://castingfrontier.com
Casting Networks, http://castingnetworks.com
Backstage, http://www.backstage.com

Some of these websites carry the same breakdowns, so I would filter through and find which work for you. The top three are Actors Access, Casting Networks, and LA Casting. When you have representation, they will generally also ask you to get an account with these domains.

Also research Showfax, an online acting community primarily known for providing sides for audition, which are largely self-submission auditions from the websites listed previously. This way, it is your responsibility to get hold of the sides yourself, and you want to be an intelligent. Know an agent will never work harder for you than you will work for yourself. It is essential for you to be self-submitting for auditions; you can't just sit at home and wait for the phone to ring, hoping your agent will do all the work—no way. Self-submitting is a great way to build your portfolio, and because you won't typically find big studio auditions on these breakdowns, you can use the auditions as a training ground to perfect your audition process and find out what works for you. This way, you'll have your auditions mastered by the time you get to the big offices.

SELF-TAPING AUDITIONS

We've all heard about actors self-taping auditions and submitting them online. Self-taping is an amazing resource. You have the ability to tape and send your audition without even leaving your living room. If casting wants you to self-tape, they will request it. Self-taping is not something you offer. It is usually requested because casting is screening the first stage of auditions via Tapes, or they are sending the tapes to a different state/country.

Auditioning on tape is very different from auditioning in person, mainly because you don't get the personal interaction with casting that you would if you were to walk into the office. However, the plus side is you can rehearse your audition and record it as many times as you want until you are satisfied with the final recording. The expectations of self-tape auditions are high, because you have had an opportunity to rehearse the scene and perfect it. Your audition tape is required to be good quality and stumble-free. You can self-tape your own auditions if you have the equipment (which these days is becoming more and more accessible), or there are professional videotaping services with a no-fuss approach.

With a professional company, you go in and have your performance recorded with professional lighting and camera equipment. They generally send you a link to your audition, and you can then send it off, or they can send it off for you. I myself use and highly recommend a company called Audition Tape in Hollywood. They have been taping actors since 2000 and offer reasonable prices and coaching if you require it for your reading.

If you're taping the audition yourself, you want to make sure you have all the technicalities in place. Have a friend come and read for you off camera. You can't read the other characters' dialogue. Then, in terms of the video composition itself, you want your video to look as professional as possible. To achieve this, you need some checkpoints:

Background. Your background should be a plain backdrop. This will ensure it doesn't distract from your performance.

Camera. Keep the camera still by using a tripod or resting it on a hard surface. Make sure you're shooting in a close-up or medium close-up range. You want the camera frame to be tight, so the focus is solely on you and your performance. A medium close-up is shot from the waist up. A close-up is shot from the shoulders up, and both of these shots should have very little headroom. Essentially, we don't need to see your legs or the walls of your place (as nice as they are, I'm sure). The casting director wants to focus on your performance, and usually they like to see the life of the character and performance through your eyes—not your legs or apartment wallpaper.

Lighting. Natural lighting is sufficient; however, if you have lighting you want to use, feel free. Just make sure it looks natural and makes you look your best by not making you look to harsh and too contrasting with your background.

Sound. This is a tricky one, because your audio needs to be clear and precise. You don't need external mics, and most cameras have built-in microphones, even iPhones do. You want your sound to be the highest quality, so make sure you have equipment with good sound capability and make sure you are recording somewhere quiet so your lines are clearly audible.

Contact information. In the video, make sure you state your contact information so casting can reach you. The best ways to do this is by using a slate at the beginning of your audition. A slate is when you state your name and what role you are reading for. Then, at the end of the video, you can put a digital insertion of your contact information, including your name, the role, your agent's contact information, or your own personal contact information if you're not yet represented. Contact information should include your phone number and e-mail address.

If you choose to go the route of self-recording rather than professional recording, a great camera that a lot of my professional actor friends and industry associates use is the Flip Video Mino. It's small and portable and is the best mini camcorder available for straight-to-web video. It's HD quality and even comes with little tripod legs you can attach. The *Wall Street Journal* called it "the market for a simple camcorder that records high-quality video."

Mossberg, Walter S. (2008-11-12). "Flip Camcorder Goes High-Def". Wall Street Journal. That's good enough for me.

So you have all your tools on how you can keep proactive career-wise, but one piece of advice I wish I'd paid more attention to when I arrived is that it's key for your sanity to aim to achieve a balanced lifestyle. Achieving balance is different for everyone. If you're a go-getter, then make time to support yourself by things as simple as taking a hot bath to relax and clear your mind. If you're at the other end of the scale and more laid-back, try being productive and scheduling more activities for yourself. (You can use the goal setting planner outlined earlier.)

Los Angeles is a known as a scattered city with hundreds of things always happening, which can steal your focus if you're not careful. Make sure you are constantly feeding your soul and staying connected with yourself so you can be the healthiest version of you. If you're a type A personality, like me, and constantly doing a million things at once, sometimes you need to slow down and relax. When I first arrived, instead of getting up to speed with Hollywood, I was running around and speeding up with Hollywood. My life lacked balance. I was so busy trying to be everything to everybody else that I forgot to think about myself and to take a breath and prioritize. I was lucky I had the opportunities to go home to New Zealand for the holidays and to organize work visas, which was a blessing in disguise, because being home offered me perspective. Lots of actors I know of have put their lives on hold because they're too busy trying to be an actor.

Ultimately, they seem to be the ones that end up trying to execute their dreams frantically by running around and then eventually become frustrated and burnt out. If life imitates art, then if you are burnt out, it will manifest itself in some form or another, whether in the audition room or in your lifestyle. Something will be affected. Think about acting as just a form of expressionism about life that is only enriched by life's experiences. Make smart actor choices and have a life to begin with.

California is known for its great lifestyle, so get out there and use all the resources available. California has sun almost all year-round, so there's no excuse to sit on the couch and be lazy. With your free time, explore places and participate in activities that make you happy. When I first arrived, I explored places I had absolutely no interest in, because people had told me they were must-see spots. The truth is, if it's not something you're interested in, then it's not something you're interested in. Use your time in a way that benefits your greater good too.

Getting out of your own head and giving back is also a great use of time and helps to keep your sanity. Charity work and volunteering is something I think every actor should invest time in. Not necessarily continuously, because we all get busy, but get involved in the community. You see so many celebrities doing charity work, and yes, most of that is organized by their publicist to create a good public image and they could care less. For the average Joe, the benefits are huge, because when you give something to someone who has nothing, it generally makes you appreciate what you have. Becoming grateful for aspects of your own life is a rewarding experience in itself. Not to mention it's great to get you out of your own head, especially if you're partial to having a pity party for yourself when things get rough. Never underestimate the power of giving back.

Nonprofit organizations have so many categories to choose from; they range from mentoring children, helping others with disabilities, working with the homeless, assisting with disaster relief, and volunteering with animal rescue to name a few areas. Then there are thousands of different kinds of charities to choose from in LA, so you don't have to sign up to something you have no interest in. Working at an animal shelter is probably not the best idea if you don't like animals. So take your time, do your research, and find out which charities feel right for you. I have worked with creative arts and education mentoring for kids with Create Now Inc. and Young Storytellers Foundation and animal rescue shelters, including No Kill LA and Ace of Hearts. Check those out for some basics to get you started, but the list is forever long.

As an actor, exploring and getting out in nature usually helps you maintain a healthy mental attitude to your work, as well offering more clarity. What if you on a budget? Well, don't worry; keeping active doesn't have to cost money either. The city has an endless list of ideas of activities.

There are some great websites that offer daily deals for businesses around LA and activities. They can be discounted down to as much as half or a quarter of the original price. Check out the sites Groupon, Living Social, and Gilt Groupe to get you started. Also use an online website called Yelp to research the businesses online—not just for these online deals but for most places in general. You're new to the city, so chances are you're unfamiliar with what the city has to offer. Yelp is a website that posts reviews of businesses, customer reviews, and ratings based on all their customer feedback. It's a great way to help you find out what is legit and what to stay away from. It will save you a lot of time, money, potential headaches, and hassle.

You can also take advantage of LA's yearlong summer and try out some of the great hiking spots. Great spots for exploring are Griffith Park, Runyon Canyon, and Malibu. They are beautiful and offer a rare chance to get out among nature in LA. Also think outside the box. You can mix it up and spend a day at the beach learning your scripts for auditions instead of sitting alone in your apartment.

Research local theatre companies, as socializing at these places can often present opportunities that can also turn into networking. Some amazing small independent theatre companies that have cheap shows with original works are The Ruskin Theatre Group in Santa Monica and Son of Semele in Silverlake. There are also California's more prominent theatre companies, such as The Geffen Playhouse and Center Theatre Group, which generally have well-established plays with often star-studded casts and tend to be on the pricier side. (They are well worth it, though, if you have the extra funds.)

If theatre isn't your thing but you like shows, check out a comedy show. Everybody loves a good laugh, and in this city, you are overwhelmed with options. Some great professional comedy shows are often held at The Laugh Factory, The Hollywood Improv, and The Comedy Store. They are really reasonably priced with tickets around ten dollars, and each place having a two-item minimum you have to order off their menu. There are also local comedy and improv schools that train many of the professional celebrity comedians in the industry right now, and they have troupes that put on shows. Check out Second City, The Groundlings Theatre, or Upright Citizens Brigade (USB).

These are a few ideas to get you started, but the options are endless. Networking is also a bonus, so in addition to getting out and about, you're meeting new people! It's essential in a new city, but it can lead to meeting like-minded people who can offer you advice and are sometimes on similar journeys as you. Most actors I know who start living their lives fully in this capacity find recreational aspects of life present encounters with like-minded artists. So seriously, utilize the resources available to you, explore, play, and research as much as possible.

I wanted to ask some industry professionals their opinion on resources in LA and how they achieve a balanced lifestyle. Here is what they told me:

MARILYN MANDEL, CASTING DIRECTOR, CSA:

Use all resources available to you. Research as much as possible. Go to the library, join community groups, small theatre companies, and network, read online articles. Backstage is a great online resource for current articles. Listen to and subscribe to KCRW. There are a million benefits, and the music is outstanding, and the news is NPR. It's the best thing about Los Angeles. The Academy Motion Pictures Arts & Sciences (the folks that bring you the Oscars) are the founders of The Margaret Herrick Library in Beverly Hills. There you can read just about any film script you can think of. Drama bookstores like Samuel French are also fabulous resources; even talking to the staff there, who are so informative and knowledgeable. Good idea to get acquainted with what's available to you, and much of it is *free*. Also a key piece of advice I would give to actors moving to Los Angeles would be to have a life. So many actors come out to Hollywood and just "try" to be actors, and they forget to live life. Actors are just artists that imitate life, and what makes an actor's work full and truthful is having a life full of curiosity and exploration. You want to constantly be digging and discovering, because your art won't be full if your life isn't full. – Marilyn Mandel (Casting director, CSA) in discussion, 2013.

ZAK SHAIKH, WRITER/COCREATOR OF
THE WARNER BROS. SERIES *SULLIVAN AND SON*, WGA:

I try to achieve balance by leaving town as often as possible, as it gives me perspective—often by going back home. On a day-to-day level, I try to instill routines, which I allow some flexibility for (so I don't feel trapped), but the routines help me be productive and feel fine about not working all the time. Morning exercise often helps me, also being social, as writing can be rather lonely. So I play football every week, which forces me to hang out with twenty-one other dudes, eleven of whom I'm generally trying to kick and cuss. Also, I read and watch a lot of upcoming shows. When I'm busy, I find that my movie-watching and TV-viewing time disappears. Reading scripts and watching shows/films is quite stimulating; not only does it give me fresh ideas, but it also helps me catch up on what everyone else is chatting about. But let's be honest, it's never a slow period is it? – Zak Shaikh (Writer, Warner Bros) in discussion, 2013.

KATT SHEA, WRITER, DIRECTOR, AND CREATOR OF
THE 1992 CULT CLASSIC FILM *POISON IVY*:

To have balance, you have to feel good about yourself. You have to love your-self so that you allow yourself to be successful. If you don't and you are suc-cessful anyway, you will self-destruct, so it's very important to work on the spirit aspect of you. As you heal your pain, you become a better actor. Many ac-tors think if they lose their pain they will lose their emotion, but it's not true. As you love yourself more and heal more your emotions, you get better control of yourself as an actor and you gain depth and connection. – Katt Shea (writer/director) in discussion, 2013.

SARAH MOSHMAN, EMMY AWARD-WINNING DIRECTOR:

Life is all about finding balance, and sometimes I feel like I have it and sometimes several aspects suffer. It depends on the show I'm working for or the project I'm passionate about at that time. I just try to remind myself to find moments of re-laxation and that stepping away from work is often the best way to refresh your creativity, especially in the edit process. What's all the hard work for if you never get to enjoy the fruits of your labor? I also try to separate home life from work life as much as I can, but in this industry, it's definitely a tall order. I try to remind myself when I'm not working how crazy-busy I get when I am working to enjoy the slow periods. Living a freelance lifestyle is tough; it's so up and down and often out of your control. I try to stay current by attending events and screenings, work on my own projects, and connect back with my goals and myself. Most importantly, I enjoy life!

Also, networking is everything in this business. The people you meet at work, at events, through friends, those could be the people that help you get where you need to go. Meeting people in person is far more effective than a faceless résumé on a website or via e-mail. I always say to myself when I'm feeling lazy and don't want to go out, "Nothing is going to happen to you tonight if you stay here and sit on the couch, but something could happen if you leave and go out." You just never know who you're going to meet when you leave your comfort zone and put yourself out there. But you'll never meet them when you stay on the couch. I go do fun things in the city, reconnect with friends I haven't seen in months, workout more consistently, enjoy the quiet time with my husband and my puppy, anything I've been meaning to do because you could get a call or e-mail and there you are back to work before you know it!

The best piece of advice I have ever given myself is as follows: "You are on your own path." I don't compare myself to anyone else. I want to have the best career trajectory for Sarah Moshman, whatever that means for me. No two people have the exact same path to success or to a job, so I think it's important to recognize and celebrate our differences. Get inspired by the people around you, and use that in your own life. – Sarah Moshman (Heartfelt Productions/ Emmy award-winning filmmaker) in discussion, 2013.

In the previous chapters, I've listed some tools and advice that have been shared with me on my path. Hopefully, it will help provide some guidance to your eventual success. Hollywood is full of people with horrible attitudes who would on stomp on your dreams to make their own a reality. It is also full of people who are positive and who would love to support and help you facilitate your dreams. Surround yourself with people who have similar goals and aspirations and have a generally positive attitude about LA.

The people who are trying to drag others down are usually doing so because of their own negative experiences. (Don't let their crap become yours.) Be positive, think optimistically, and surround yourself with positive people who inspire you. Surrounding yourself with positivity is a huge factor to creating a successful environment, but it's hard getting started. You might need to reach out.

In this business, people sometimes feel ashamed to be vulnerable because they see asking for advice as a sign of weakness. In truth, it's a sign of strength. Things won't happen overnight, and actors (myself included) are often too proud to ask for help. Because of this, I'm going to emphasize that not reaching out is usually because of pride, which is driven by your ego. Don't let your ego drive you; be humble and ask for guidance if you need it. I learned this by never wanting to take something from someone and feel that I owed the person something in return. I see now they were offering me a gift, because they wouldn't have offered their help or advice if they didn't believe in me. The fact that I didn't take it was ultimately because I didn't feel I deserved it. Looking back, I sometimes wish I'd taken different offers, because some could have led to great opportunities. Don't be too modest to ask for assistance. Successful individuals established their careers with a supportive network. Very few things happened from one person alone. Think about it—we even come into the world from the creation of two people (if you get what I mean), so never be ashamed to reach out.

Even if the question is as small as to ask which streets to take to avoid traffic. A gem of advice however small may help keep you on time and as a result book that audition. On that note, one piece of advice that has helped me more than anything when travelling between castings and which I remind myself of every day when I get behind the wheel in LA.

In the words of the amazing Bette Davis: When asked by Johnny Carson,

"What is the best way an aspiring starlet could get into Hollywood?",

Ms. Davis replied, "Take fountain!"

Naturally, there are also no absolutes in this business, and everyone in this industry has a different view. Much of the advice stated in this book is based on opinion, my own and those of industry professionals. You may totally disregard it all of it if you wish. Hollywood has no rule book (although sometimes we all wish it did), but there is some common sense and general consensus that is worthy advice, and statistics show that help increase your chances of success.

You are never alone, I wanted to create a continued support network for you after you read this book, so I have created a sister website - hometohollywood.com - so you can always have a resource to refer to. It will help provide a network with constant updated material on resources, ranging from industry businesses to social happenings around the city. Home to Hollywood will also be available for direct contact through our website via. email (info@hometohollywood.com). Ultimately, because we've all made the journey we want to help and guide you as much as possible so you can facilitate yours!

I have one remaining thought I want to leave you with: Please don't worry so much. You're not the first person to move to LA, and practically everyone here is a transplant and had to go through the same growing pains. Take a deep breath, congratulate yourself for taking the steps toward your dreams, and relax. I wish you the best success. Ultimately, this is your journey, and you choose how it is going to happen. But this is the city of imagination, and if you have the vision and you are willing to work harder than everyone else to achieve it, then this is your town to do it. Los Angeles has the best and worst of all worlds possible, and Hollywood is what you make of it. Make it a positive journey. Make Hollywood your home.

Disclaimer: This booklet is providing advice only, and the author is in no way responsible for any action taken based on this advice. *Home to Hollywood* cannot in any way be held responsible for or accountable for any loss or damages that may result from any actions taken following the advice or recommendations provided.

NOTES

NOTES

NOTES

NOTES

THANK YOU'S

Contributors:

Zak Shaikh

Sarah Moshman

Katt Shea

Marilyn Mandel

Holly Lebed

Melissa Molina

General:

Mum

Dad

Gabby

Printed in the United States
By Bookmasters